BUILD THEE MORE STATELY MANSIONS

Participatory Foresight and the Mid-Century U.S. Economy

Steven W. Popper, Richard Silberglitt, Fabian Villalobos,
Khrystyna Holynska, Krystyna Marcinek,
Nadia Almasalkhi, Jack Lashendock

Prepared for the Defense Advanced Research Projects Agency
Approved for public release; distribution is unlimited

RAND NATIONAL DEFENSE RESEARCH INSTITUTE

For more information on this publication, visit **www.rand.org/t/RRA1947-2**.

About RAND

The RAND Corporation is a research organization that develops solutions to public policy challenges to help make communities throughout the world safer and more secure, healthier and more prosperous. RAND is nonprofit, nonpartisan, and committed to the public interest. To learn more about RAND, visit www.rand.org.

Research Integrity

Our mission to help improve policy and decisionmaking through research and analysis is enabled through our core values of quality and objectivity and our unwavering commitment to the highest level of integrity and ethical behavior. To help ensure our research and analysis are rigorous, objective, and nonpartisan, we subject our research publications to a robust and exacting quality-assurance process; avoid both the appearance and reality of financial and other conflicts of interest through staff training, project screening, and a policy of mandatory disclosure; and pursue transparency in our research engagements through our commitment to the open publication of our research findings and recommendations, disclosure of the source of funding of published research, and policies to ensure intellectual independence. For more information, visit www.rand.org/about/principles.

RAND's publications do not necessarily reflect the opinions of its research clients and sponsors.

Published by the RAND Corporation, Santa Monica, Calif.

Library of Congress Cataloging-in-Publication Data is available for this publication.

ISBN: 978-1-9774-1469-4

Cover: Illustration by Sara Herbst/RAND, Yevhenii/Adobe Stock and royyimzy/Adobe Stock

About This Report

U.S.-China competition, including economic competition, has come to define U.S. foreign policy since 2017. The two economies are the first- and second-largest national economies in the world and they are deeply intertwined in all aspects of international exchange. Any changes to the relationship, however necessary, could be costly.

To respond to this challenge, RAND conducted economic and institutional analyses of U.S.-China competition, engaged in a participatory foresight exercise to understand the long-term path for ensuring U.S. economic health, and created two economic competition games exploring the dynamics of multiple countries trying to ensure their economic health while interacting with each other and the private sector. This report, the second of a four-part series, presents the results of the participatory foresight exercise designed to understand the path for ensuring long-term U.S. economic health. Part 1 presents the economic and institutional analyses of U.S.-China economic competition. Parts 3 and 4 describe two economic competition games that explore the dynamics of multiple countries trying to ensure their own economic health while interacting with one another and the private sector.

In this report, we provide an overview of findings derived from workshops conducted in June 2023 to examine (1) what the mid-century U.S. economy will need to be in order to be able to meet the requirements of both domestic needs and national security in a future characterized by strategic competition and (2) what possible pathways can be created for achieving that vision. In addition to the substantive findings, we also illustrate the potential value of the Vision, Strategic Concepts, Assumptions, Robust Pathways (VSCARP) approach to participatory foresight. VSCARP is designed to support meaningful strategic deliberations among participants with diverging interests, perspectives, and assumptions about the future. Its results are agreed-on, robust courses of action that take into account varied interests while providing pathways toward a common future vision. VSCARP also provides participants with a vocabulary to sustain ongoing interagency and intercommunity process across a future of dynamic change.

This report will be relevant to those who have interest in future directions of the U.S. economy and societal welfare, defense economics, participatory foresight, strategic planning, and decisionmaking under deep uncertainty.

The views, opinions and/or findings expressed are those of the authors and should not be interpreted as representing the official views or policies of the Department of Defense or the U.S. government.

RAND National Security Research Division

This research was sponsored by the Defense Advanced Research Projects Agency and conducted within the Acquisition and Technology Policy Program of the RAND National

Security Research Division (NSRD), which operates the National Defense Research Institute (NDRI), a federally funded research and development center sponsored by the Office of the Secretary of Defense, the Joint Staff, the Unified Combatant Commands, the Navy, the Marine Corps, the defense agencies, and the defense intelligence enterprise.

For more information on the RAND Acquisition and Technology Policy Program, see www.rand.org/nsrd/atp or contact the director (contact information is provided on the webpage).

Acknowledgments

We thank Whitney Mason, director of the Defense Advanced Research Projects Agency (DARPA) Microsystems Technology Office, for overall guidance and feedback on this project; Michael Dambach and Paul Dietrich, both of DARPA, for further support; Anne Fischer, formerly deputy director of DARPA's Defense Sciences Office, for guiding an early iteration of this project; Joel Predd of RAND for leading that early iteration and co-conceiving of the project; and Caolionn O'Connell, formerly of RAND and now at the Aerospace Corporation, for co-conceiving of the project.

We are extremely grateful to the participants in both workshops for their willingness to engage freely in discussions and their insights that provided the basis for the analysis and results described in Chapters 2 and 3.

We derived considerable benefit from the formal peer reviews provided by Jonathan Welburn of RAND and Henry E. Brady, Class of 1941 Monroe Deutsch Professor of Political Science and Public Policy in the Goldman School of Public Policy at the University of California, Berkeley. The report was considerably improved by their contributions; all remaining errors or omissions are our sole responsibility.

We also thank production editor Matt Byrd, editors Dan Cabrera and Stephanie Lonsinger, and graphic designer D. Carol Ponce for their skillful assistance.

Summary

What vision would provide the basis for a mid-century U.S. economy that will meet domestic needs, sustain national security, and operate effectively in a global economy characterized by strategic competition? And what are the available policy pathways for achieving that vision? In this report, we present the principal findings of an exploratory analysis to apply participatory foresight to both questions. The approach was to bring together a diverse group of experts and challenge them to envision future states of the U.S. economy in 2040, along with alternative pathways toward different U.S. futures, through a series of structured discussions across several workshops.

These questions arose as part of a broader project in which the Defense Advanced Research Projects Agency asked RAND to respond to the following question: *How can the United States ensure that its economy meets the nation's needs under conditions of coupled, strategic competition?* Overall project aims included exploring the proactive steps that can be taken to ensure a healthy U.S. economy over the long term, what that economy might look like in 2040, and whether this vision can be achieved in a way that does not necessarily hamper the Chinese economy but rather benefits both the United States *and* China.

To respond to that challenge, RAND researchers engaged in an economic and institutional analysis of U.S.-China competition, conducted the participatory foresight exercise discussed in this report, and created economic competition games exploring the dynamics of multiple countries trying to ensure their economic health while interacting with one another and the private sector. Forthcoming RAND studies of U.S.-China economic competition capture the results of the economic and institutional analyses and the games.

The Participatory Foresight Workshops

The workshops were structured using the Vision, Strategic Concepts, Assumptions, Robust Pathways (VSCARP) approach to participatory foresight, first employed in a 2018 National Safety Council and RAND report, *The Road to Zero: A Vision for Achieving Zero Roadway Deaths by 2050*. VSCARP employs a suite of foresight methods with a policy analytic overlay. The intent is to support deliberations across interests and beliefs under conditions of deep uncertainty. VSCARP mainly draws on the following methods:

- **Backcasting,** as contrasted with forecasting—in which the past and present are projected into the future—starts with participants describing the main features of a desirable *future* U.S. economy and then works backward to ask how to get to that state: What makes that future state stable? What trade-offs were required to get there? What happened to make it feasible? What did not happen? Who was involved in realizing that future?

- **Three Horizon Foresight** is used to contrast some described future (3rd Horizon) with the present (1st Horizon) to draw insights for then considering viable alternative pathways across the 2nd Horizon, the intermediate period, toward the envisioned future.
- **Assumption-based planning** supports a deconflicted, side-by-side comparison of alternatives by detecting key load-bearing assumptions for each strategy (that is, assumptions such that their failure would require significant changes in plans for the future). The analysis then identifies where potential vulnerabilities might arise, what hedging or shaping actions might be employed to reduce vulnerability, and what early warning signals (or *signposts*) should be monitored.
- **Scenarios**—groups of structured narratives of policies, trends, and outcomes—which emerge not as ends in themselves but rather as tools to elicit insights into alternative courses of action, leading indicators to monitor, and important decision or transfer points among strategies in light of unfolding events.

The focus of this report is on the second of the two workshops.

Workshop Themes

The workshops were carried out at a small scale with compressed timing and with necessarily limited participation. Nevertheless, several themes emerged that suggest what could be endorsed by a wider, broader, and more intense effort using the same approach:

- **Vision.** There exist important elements of a vision for a desirable mid-century U.S. economy that can receive endorsement among individuals and across groups possessing different interests, perceptions, worldviews, and sets of assumptions.
- **Obstacles.** Domestic policies and actions can enable movement toward or provide barriers to reaching desirable U.S. economic futures. This recognition restores a sense of agency that contrasts with recent perceptions of governmental incapacity to effect meaningful change.
- **Forks in the road.** Important nodes along several defined pathways include (1) the capacity for future U.S. investment, both foreign and domestic, (2) the need to plan and provide political framing for, consensus on, and strategic goals of such investment, and (3) effective management of the relationship with China for the benefit of both countries and the globe—an outcome that is not solely determined by U.S. actions.
- **External relations.** Strong relationships with allies and outreach to emerging economies that is not primarily couched in terms of the U.S.-China strategic competition can support movement toward desirable U.S. economic futures.

Participants explored what might constitute a robust approach for achieving elements of the 2040 vision. The suggested short-term actions reflected two principal concerns:

- China can best be managed through a slow, deliberate approach that looks for reciprocal signals and actions. This was judged as low regret because of the ability to tune deterrence to appropriate levels and because such measures usually do not stir partisan domestic concerns.
- There was general agreement on the need for reframing budget processes in the context of both constitutional authorities and the realities of the modern age. A bipartisan commission could consider the budget process as well as incentives for politicians to recommit to governance and stewardship.

Workshop Process Outcomes

Several key process (as opposed to product) outcomes emerged that suggest the potential for further deliberations in which the VSCARP approach can be employed at a larger scale of engagement and with a greater capacity for deliberation and meaningful multiparty interaction:

- **Complexities made observable.** It is possible to elaborate complex relationships across time, policy domains, and categories of interest and share them in a manner designed to enhance a collective ability to observe them.
- **Structure for dynamic deliberation.** A systematic, structured process can enable groups of individuals with highly varied training and expertise to think dynamically across an evolving domestic and international landscape in which each successive period possesses changing requirements for success.
- **Assumptions and strategic alternatives.** A process exists for sharing alternative strategic concepts; examining them simultaneously for key assumptions, vulnerabilities, and performance outcomes; and, moreover, identifying for each strategy signpost indicators for monitoring, shaping strategies to enhance the prospects for success, and hedging actions to limit downside risks.
- **Deliberation with analysis.** Participatory foresight can provide an important element within a larger framing to provide deliberation with analysis as the entry point for more-detailed integration of policy deliberation with analytical decision support.

Beyond these immediate findings, the VSCARP approach can serve as the basis for a larger, more-detailed deliberation with analysis effort along these lines, as well as in application to other issues involving the intersection of complicated systems; the presence of different stakeholders, office holders, and their individual and organizational perspectives; and considerable uncertainty about trends, causal links, and potentially conflicting priorities.

Contents

Figures and Tables

Figures

Tables

CHAPTER 1

Viewing Through a Glass Darkly

Build thee more stately mansions, O my soul,
As the swift seasons roll!
Leave thy low-vaulted past!
Let each new temple, nobler than the last,
Shut thee from heaven with a dome more vast,
Till thou at length art free,
Leaving thine outgrown shell by life's unresting sea!

— "The Chambered Nautilus," Oliver Wendell Holmes (1858)

As with Holmes's chambered nautilus, the economic system of America's future is currently being shaped and crafted with each passing day. What economy does the United States require by mid-century to meet its domestic needs, support national security, and operate effectively in a global environment characterized by strategic competition? How does the United States anticipate and limit the effects of deleterious actions by potential adversaries (to whom it is, in varying degrees, bound by economic ties) while having its policies find acceptance from allies, partners, and important nonaligned states?

The notion of bringing such an economy into being by plotting out a strategically coherent course of short- and medium-term actions would appear to be ludicrous given the myriad complexities involved, the potential for trend shifts and surprising discontinuities, and the certainty of any attempt at predictive forecasting being confounded by the reality that ultimately unfolds. And yet, a sequential course of policy actions will certainly evolve, even if only as the result of measures taken to address short-term exigencies and perceived concerns. That course of action, intentionally or not, will also shape *de facto* the U.S. economic machinery in 2040.[1] It would be desirable, if possible, to fashion a lens that would make it more feasible to consider those short-term actions within a strategic perspective.

The issue framed in this report can be decomposed into two parts: What is a vision for the U.S. economy in 2040 that meets the stated criteria? And what are the available policy

[1] The selected year should be viewed as being more representative than precise. It is far enough from the present (2024) as to suggest the feasibility of several alternative policy courses while at the same time being sufficiently near as to not make some incredible presumption of a degree of continuity with present processes, institutions, and trends.

pathways for achieving that vision? This report presents the principal findings of an exploratory analysis to apply participatory foresight to both questions. The approach was to bring together a diverse group of experts from several fields (economics, geopolitics, technology, and trade) and challenge them to envision future states of the U.S. economy in 2040, along with diverse pathways toward different U.S. futures, through a series of structured discussions across several days of workshops.[2]

As an exploratory analysis, the workshops were carried out at a small scale with compressed timing and with necessarily limited participation. Therefore, the analysis provides a foundation that is too narrow to draw strong conclusions, make firm recommendations, or establish unassailable guidelines. However, the value of the effort was twofold: On the one hand, it provided a test of a specific process in which experts and stakeholders can engage in structured discussion about potential pathways to desirable futures, and on the other, it provided an initial basis for addressing the two principal questions regarding the U.S. economy in 2040.

The first workshop in the series was conducted with RAND experts to gain insight on the evolving U.S. relationships with other countries. The workshop's findings detailed how countries around the world might react to U.S. policies, especially the edge cases for which the benefits of cooperation were not obvious. The workshop highlighted that other countries would act according to their own national interests and dependent on how cooperation with or opposition to the United States—even when costly—would benefit them, especially if a lack of cooperation or a lack of opposition would be even more costly. A highly condensed list of findings was prepared for the second workshop and reviewed to assist in informing the analysis prepared for this report.

The second of the two workshops, described in Appendix A, was held in person at RAND's Arlington, Virginia, office on June 23–24, 2023, and is the focus of this report. The process of the workshop was based on several core principles:

- **Problematic prediction.** Uncertainty will remain a factor that we cannot forecast our way out of.
- **Heterogeneity.** Among U.S. stakeholders, there are differing interests, equities, and perspectives. Operating globally requires considering views of others outside the United States.
- **A focus on framing solutions rather than on limiting assumptions.** Rather than argue over which currently unknowable assumptions about the future might prove to be true, focus instead on finding courses of action that
  - achieve some degree of consensus over short-term, "low-regret" actions that might be robust against a variety of risks
  - detail the process of adjudicating future trade-offs over the longer term depending on newer information, in effect changing course from the short-term, low-regret actions if useful

[2] A short overview of the series of workshops is found in Appendix A. This also includes a list of attendees and their institutional affiliations.

- might prove to be robust—that is, courses of action that are designed to achieve satisfactory outcomes for policy objectives across a spectrum of potential future trends, events, and adversarial actions.

- **Enhanced visibility.** Bring out important juxtapositions, central themes, and strategic and policy alternatives by making them explicit.

The workshops were structured using the Vision, Strategic Concepts, Assumptions, Robust Pathways (VSCARP) approach to participatory foresight.[3] VSCARP employs an integrated stream of several foresight methods with a policy analytic overlay. It mainly draws on the following methods:

- **Backcasting,** as contrasted with forecasting—in which the past and present are projected into the future—starts with participants describing the main features of a desirable future U.S. economy and then works backward to ask how to get to that state: What makes that future state stable? What trade-offs were required? What happened to make it feasible? What did *not* happen? Who was involved in realizing that future?[4]
- **Three Horizon Foresight** is used to contrast some described future (3rd Horizon) with the present (1st Horizon) to draw insights for then considering viable alternative pathways across the 2nd Horizon, the intermediate period, toward the envisioned future. The value of Three Horizon Foresight is to create dynamic mapping across time, as well as cause and effect, to frame the entire VSCARP structure.
- **Assumption-based planning** to support a deconflicted, side-by-side comparison of alternatives by detecting key load-bearing assumptions (that is, assumptions such that their failure would require significant changes in plans for the future) for each strategy. The analysis then identifies
  - where potential vulnerabilities might arise
  - hedging actions to reduce consequences of possibly broken assumptions
  - shaping actions to affect the future environment and reduce vulnerability
  - early warning signals (or *signposts*) to be monitored to determine if change is necessary.
- **Scenarios,** groups of structured narratives of policies, trends, and future outcomes. Scenarios emerge from the prior steps in VSCARP and are not considered ends in themselves but rather as tools to elicit insights regarding the alternative courses of action, key indicators to monitor, and important decision or transfer points among strategies in light of unfolding events.

[3] First employed in the Road to Zero strategic planning process, VSCARP has since been applied to an increasingly wide set of policy settings (Liisa Ecola, Steven W. Popper, Richard Silberglitt, and Laura Fraade-Blanar, *The Road to Zero: A Vision for Achieving Zero Roadway Deaths by 2050*, RAND Corporation, RR-2333-NSC, 2018).

[4] Envisioning the future is difficult. The context of the present overpowers the imagination, and the multiplicity of futures is daunting. It is easier to be placed in a future and look backward.

The Vision, Strategic Concepts, Assumptions, Robust Pathways (VSCARP) Method

Table 1.1 provides a capsule view of the structure behind the workshops. The left-most column shows the various steps or stages of the process. The next column shows the principal outputs received from that step. This report highlights only the major outputs generated during the intermediary steps, but the table demonstrates how conclusions were derived incrementally. There follow two columns with directional arrows. Taken together, the columns provide a flowchart of the VSCARP process and detail the points at which the process uses the respective strengths of both small-group and large-group dynamics. Generally, the small groups were used as both incubators of ideas and devices for achieving engagement. (Experience suggests that in a group of three to five people confronted with a collective challenge, even individuals who typically shy from speaking more openly find the comfort and encouragement to participate actively.) The larger groups helped with comparison, sorting, and eventual incorporation of the contributions made in the small groups. This process also generated new material and insights that could also be incorporated into the larger framework.

The final column shows the methods that provided the theoretical and practical foundation on which the workshop and its steps were based. There is a rich literature and body of prior applications for each one. Yet using them as an integrated suite of tools generates the added value of VSCARP. Often, scenarios are used almost as an end in themselves. Writing scenarios demonstrates organizational due diligence in thinking about the future. But scenarios are often left as the end product of such reflection. If so, they become difficult to use in informing operational or even strategic decisions. There is also the further problem of how best to determine, precisely, which scenarios will best inform the decisions to be made at each level. In VSCARP, scenarios arise from prior interactions of visions and goals, opportunities and obstacles, and ways and means. It then becomes clear why those particular scenarios are considered. The scenarios, in turn, become instruments for achieving the further step of elucidation and interrogation of proposed alternative courses of action in search of framing an agreed-on, robust pathway for moving forward.

TABLE 1.1
Flow of the Vision, Strategic Concepts, Assumptions, Robust Pathways (VSCARP) Process

Step	Output	Small Groups	Plenary	Method
Describe the world of 2040 prompted by provided cues[a]	• Elements of a vision for a desirable future state in 2040 • Disruption and exploration of current worldviews	↓		Backcasting
Compare the described 2040 future state with the present	• Reveal present and prospective trade-offs and costs • Illuminate obstacles, barriers, and opportunities	→	↓	Three Horizon Foresight
Sketch out an initial agreed-on draft vision for 2040	• Assess several visions for commonalities • Formulate an agreed-on, common future vision		↙	Three Horizon Foresight
Develop strategies and pathways to the 2040 vision	• Alternative "Big Idea" strategic concepts • Agreed-on set of alternative candidate strategies for forging pathways toward the future 2040 vision	→	↙	Assumption-based planning
Identify key assumptions	• Flesh out characteristics of each strategic concept • Elicit explicit and implicit assumptions for each strategic concept • Determine key assumptions for each strategic concept	↓		Assumption-based planning
Identify vulnerabilities, signposts, and hedging and shaping actions	• Events and trends that break key strategic concept assumptions • Early warning signals of stressful trends or events • Hedging actions to limit damage • Shaping actions to create more-conducive future states	→	↓	Assumption-based planning
Map scenario pathways to future states	• Frame scenarios of outcomes as tools to elicit discussion of pathways and switch points		↓	Scenario planning
Identify guidelines for robust pathway(s) toward the 2040 vision	• Agreed-on pathway(s), signposts, hedging and shaping actions, with potential switch points		↓	Assumption-based planning

NOTE: A downward arrow (↓) indicates movement to the next step at the same group scale. A horizontal arrow (→) indicates flow from small-group to plenary discussion of the same step. A diagonal arrow (↙) indicates moving from a plenary discussion at the current step to a small-group discussion to initiate the next step.

[a] In the workshops, some groups were asked to outline a desirable future, while another was prompted to describe an undesirable future for the United States economy of 2040.

In this report, we do not draw on the rich existing literature covering myriad issues touched on during the workshop. The results being presented in this report are based on the actual content of the conversations by participants who are well familiar with that literature. The research team took outputs generated through the VSCARP process as inputs to develop this report. We therefore report workshop discussions and outputs and a structure that was then crafted from these elements. In developing the structure, we sought to preserve the essence of the deliberations while placing them in a more accessible and efficient format.

The results reported in this document are themselves of interest, even though they were produced by a small-scale single exercise. Beyond these immediate findings, the VSCARP approach can serve as the basis for a larger, more detailed *deliberation with analysis* effort along these lines, as well as in application to other issues involving the intersection of complicated systems; the presence of different stakeholders, office holders, and their individual and organizational perspectives; and considerable uncertainty about trends, causal links, and potentially conflicting priorities.

CHAPTER 2

Strategic Guidance Toward the Mid-Century Vision

Discussions of strategy often begin with laying out alternatives for action. This can sometimes be an error. Unless there has been prior, detailed discussion and agreement of what a desirable future would look like, it is difficult to engage meaningfully in selecting among strategic alternatives; what are the metrics by which alternative outcomes will be compared? Furthermore, participants who, at the beginning of the strategic planning process might all nod heads in agreement with a simple vision statement being offered, might discover uncomfortably late in the process that the same words mean different things to different stakeholders. The first challenge for the VSCARP process was to describe a generally agreed-on and reasonably detailed vision for the U.S. economy toward mid-century.

This can be a challenge, indeed. To speak of a common vision for a country as broadly diverse as the United States, and for as complex a system of complex systems as is its economy, is a daunting prospect. Yet, although no one small group can presume to provide a definitive vision, it is possible to describe what might be the major *elements* of such a vision. The VSCARP process included exposing small working groups of three to five participants to backcast from different favorable and unfavorable mid-century U.S. futures and reason backward. The groups described the characteristics of that future United States, what happened (and what did not happen) to generate that outcome, what trade-offs had been made to sustain it, and how different groups were affected along the way.

The workshop discussion coalesced on nine major desiderata by which any future outcomes could be assessed:

- human capital development and job mobility for improved well-being and access to opportunity across all population groups and generations in the United States and in U.S. partner countries
- an economy that is environmentally sustainable
- currency stability with low-cost access to capital for financing sustainable policy and growth
- access for U.S. citizens to uncorrupted international information systems with strong cybersecurity to enhance productivity
- low volatility and limited concerns about U.S. access to resources, inputs, and markets

- access to sources for ensuring and maintaining scientific and technological leadership and national security across a gamut of capabilities
- means to prevent technological information leaks to potential adversaries that would detract from U.S. security
- strong economic and security mutual interests, agreements, and treaties between the United States and partner countries
- effective connectivity and flow of people to allow innovative interactions, research and development activity, and migration, while controlling nefarious activities.

The discussions suggested that beyond the strictly economic factors, important political and societal outcomes would need to ensue from these conditions. Any successful society needs an effective civil society and government. U.S. civil society and government are challenged to meet several needs. Those voiced most frequently in the small-scale breakout working groups when brought to a plenary discussion (Step 3 in Table 1.1) were needs to

- reduce disinformation and the ensuing polarization of the electorate
- enhance social cohesion and achieve sufficient levels of trust
- sustain education, at all levels, designed for meeting present and future needs
- move away from budgetary imbalance and financial brinksmanship
- recognize the importance of effective governance and providing it
- achieve sustainable growth balanced with equitable distribution.

These, along with the more strictly economic components, became important features of a common vision for the U.S. economy in 2040 and for framing strategic alternatives to achieve them.

The question remained open of which among a variety of potential pathway would bring the United States closest to this ideal. In part, the difference in views stemmed from assumptions surrounding presently unanswerable questions about what current trends will hold up, shift, or be replaced by new realities over the course of the next few decades. These views would then affect how feasible one might perceive different strategies to be. A second factor leading to alternative strategic concepts was that of priority and emphasis. Some attendees focused more on affecting the standing of the U.S. economy internationally while others placed emphasis on how well the U.S. economy served domestic needs. Different normative valuations of those needs in turn led to further dispersion.

Once again placed into small groups (Step 4), the attendees generated some 15 alternative strategic concepts around which they could envision a coherent strategy being framed to fulfill elements of the 2040 vision for the U.S. economy.[1] The goal at this point of VSCARP is to

[1] The breakout groups were encouraged to think of Big Ideas or "bumper stickers" that would briefly describe each strategy within a spectrum of possible strategies. In reality, such simplistic strategic concepts rarely see implementation in their pure form. There is always give and take, and elements from different strategic concepts are melded into a composite to guide courses of action and policies in many issue areas.

produce a spectrum of internally consistent (but by no means comprehensive) alternatives for investigation. When the groups were brought back to plenary for comparison, it became clear that the strategic concepts could be amalgamated into five distinct themes and still incorporate the output that emerged from earlier stages of the VSCARP process. Table 2.1 presents the main features among this set of five strategic concepts intended to bring the United States to realization of the envisioned U.S. economy. The five strategic concepts are not scenarios. Rather, Table 2.1 presents the tall tentpole of ideas for guiding policies and actions to carry out under each strategic concept.[2]

TABLE 2.1

Five Strategic Concepts for Achieving the 2040 Vision for the U.S. Economy

Global America	Ecosystem America	Coherent America	Supportive America	Solvent America
The U.S.-China relationship is governed by cooperation, not competition. There is a "peace dividend" for broad-based development at home. The United States conducts outreach to the Global South to foster development toward better integration into the global economy.	The United States is the center of a mutually beneficial economic network. The United States attracts the global best and brightest. Domestic education, training, and skill development are priorities. The United States and China compete to the top, not to the bottom. There is an economic NATO, or aligned trading bloc, that expands to members of MERCOSUR/L, TPP, and T-TIP.	There is more engaged and strategic policy development. Government is more responsive and effective. Big projects and big ideas unite Americans (e.g., mitigating climate change, ensuring food security). There is shared prosperity; Americans are united on shared principles of democracy and civic values. The government and private sector address misinformation.	The middle class expands. There is affordable education and health care. The government closes tax loopholes. The government and public develop and support the social safety net. There is an increase in social cohesion. Domestic education, training, and skill development are priorities.	There is a digital U.S. dollar along with DLT contracts to yield transparency and accountability. The United States is fiscally sustainable. The United States has a strategic, prioritized budget reflecting the public's values and interests. The budget process reflects existing realities.

NOTE: DLT = distributed ledger technology (e.g., blockchain); NATO = North Atlantic Treaty Organization; MERCOSUR/L = Mercado Común del Sur/Mercado Comum do Sul (the Southern Common Market, a trade bloc of South American countries); TPP = Trans-Pacific Partnership; T-TIP = Transatlantic Trade and Investment Partnership.

But at this early stage, it was analytically expedient to consider the concepts' pure forms to determine what obstacles, opportunities, or trade-offs might arise for each. This insight could then provide support to the process of hybridization among competing strategies to enhance the robustness of an overall guiding strategy that can serve as the basis for further planning and implementation.

[2] Table 2.1 by no means captures the full variety of accompanying discussion and elaboration from the workshop.

Two of the five strategic concepts (Global America and Ecosystem America) place more emphasis on the international arena. Although they both also are dependent on domestic social cohesion, fiscal sustainability, and expanding the middle class, their main emphases revolve around U.S.-China relations and the U.S. ability to maintain its place in the international order. That said, consideration of China was not absent from the other three alternatives because of its indirect relation to U.S. budgeting and strategic priorities.

Table 2.1 presents these five overarching strategic concepts in the terms their advocates would use. As seen later, these propositions and the assumptions behind them were subject to greater scrutiny in Steps 5 and 6 of the VSCARP process.

The first strategic concept, **Global America,** is built on a view that both the United States and China will understand that they need each other to prosper. This concept is cognizant that the Chinese economy is increasingly consequential for the United States, unlike the Soviet Union's economy during the Cold War. Strategic competition will still permit the exploitation of mutually beneficial cooperation in the areas in which both countries could benefit while also maintaining the entrepreneurial spirit driving both countries in a *co-opetition,* or a race to the top. This will give the United States a *peace dividend,* which can be spent on domestic initiatives.

The reaction of U.S. allies and partners to Global America might be two-fold. They might welcome a more peaceful world and the ability to focus on their domestic development. They might also appreciate an opportunity to cooperate with China, capitalizing on access to its market. However, they might have different perceptions from the security standpoint. If the United States lessens competition with China, partner defense capabilities and cooperation might be less of a priority for the United States. Thus, this strategy is built on the assumption that the allies and partners would see benefits exceeding the costs. Alternatively, the United States can offer some incentives in return for partner buy-in. The rest of the world is likely to be supportive because they would no longer need to choose between two camps and might pursue cooperation with both great powers.

The ability to pursue the Global America strategy is also built on several assumptions regarding the domestic situation. Continuing disunity and polarization of U.S. society might be so strong that only responding to an external threat can provide national cohesion. Although the Global America strategy does not involve the United States giving up global prominence (the concept relies on the assumption that the United States would remain a rule and standard setter in the international arena), its stance might be perceived as acquiescent to potential adversaries. Thus, a certain level of consent and understanding from the U.S. population and political establishment is essential to sustain this policy.

Global America is an aspirational strategy. Its realization depends on many moving parts coming together. China's own actions and postures will also determine the balance. Therefore, the United States should have a hedging approach in case China does not cooperate, the U.S. public does not support friendly relations with China, U.S. allies protest, or other countervailing forces stymie this strategy.

Ecosystem America, although a strategic concept in its own right, might be perceived also as a "floor" to fall back on if the efforts to build a global presence through cooperation prove futile. The concept focuses on further strengthening and widening a U.S.-led bloc of allies and partners. This entails continued and deepened military cooperation and the development of similar infrastructure in the economic domain. An *economic NATO*, or aligned trading bloc, should be created with clear rules and standards for those who qualify and an open door for those wishing to join. The U.S. economy would remain strong and benefit from friend-shoring and other cooperation policies with its closest circle of partners. The economic NATO might give a strong impetus for innovation because the United States would continue to be the preferred place for education and research, attracting legal immigration among the best and the brightest as well as foreign investments while maintaining the strong position of the dollar.

The rest of the world would then choose between aligning with the United States or with China. But the United States can build a system of incentives for those willing to meet the requirements and join the economic bloc. Countries other than existing U.S. close partners would receive support on this path. The fruits from economic development, brought about by dynamic cooperation of strong, innovative economies, can then be used for domestic initiatives, which is likely to bring the support of the public.

The other three strategic concepts place their focus on the domestic dimension that the first two strategic concepts treat principally as prerequisites. They prioritize domestic developments that might help the U.S. economy prosper while, at the same time, recognizing that global developments might require strategic prioritization. The tenet of these concepts is that putting the domestic house in order will better place the United States internationally. The recurring themes are of regained social cohesion within U.S. society, trust in government, and trust in one another.

Coherent America is principally focused on engineering ways to build consensus on national actions. A large-scale political mobilization, the next American *moonshot* (that is, a significant achievement in technology, energy, climate change, or other fields) can facilitate social cohesion, bringing back the feeling of national pride and trust in government and society. A more gradual path toward building social cohesion can lie through finding effective tools to counter disinformation (as a major cause of societal polarization), improving the education system to provide everyone with opportunities they want to pursue, developing a working immigration system that can help the United States solve its demographic issues in a form acceptable to the majority of the public, and increasing the efficiency and responsiveness of government. The inability to achieve any of these components might push the United States back to the less optimistic futures. The impetus to put differences in perspective can also come from the international sphere. Regardless of whether U.S.-China relations continue to be defined by strategic competition, the challenge represented by China can be used to unite U.S. society in the face of a common adversary.

The Supportive America strategic concept is also dependent on the level of social cohesion and trust in the government and society. Although not a main goal, unity is needed to achieve the objectives important for this strategic concept. The Coherent America strategy might serve as a prerequisite for this strategy. Supportive America is based on the assumption that U.S. prosperity in the past became possible because of the strong middle class. Inequitable access to resources and opportunities affects all parts of society, ultimately leading to a race to the bottom. Equity-oriented interventions (such as building a strong social safety net) need to be implemented to maintain and enhance wellsprings of growth.

This could be a costly strategy that would require increased spending in some areas and cutting spending in others, as well as larger taxes and reform of the tax system to close existing loopholes. Such decisions require political cooperation across the aisle—once again highlighting the importance of first reaching at least some level of the unity that is the emphasis of Coherent America. Although the image of the future that this strategy paints might seem attractive to many, the short- and mid-term measures, such as spending cuts, might not be acceptable to some groups and politicians representing them.

Supportive America might require fiscal responsibility and strategic budgetary planning. The **Solvent America** strategic concept aims at fiscal transparency and sustainability that can address this problem and install a more effective system of budgetary planning. The concept might also be a prerequisite in some degree for Coherent America and Supportive America. This hints at the potential for hybridization across concepts, which we address in Chapter 3.

Reshaping budgetary decisions to reduce the scale of extra-budgetary political influence can eliminate some of the incentives to capitalize on disunity and polarization. This would be aided by several new technologies, amounting to a "digital dollar" that would make it easier to deal transparently and efficiently with budgets and budgeting. Solvent America could also conceivably be triggered by a *black swan event*, or an unexpected event with major repercussions, such as a financial crisis; an alternative currency pushing the dollar out of its position as the preferred global means of reserve and settlement; a loss of confidence in U.S.-backed securities; or other events that reduce confidence in U.S. finances. Whether the U.S. government proves capable of dealing with the turmoil caused by such an event, it might ultimately increase the level of social cohesion and trust, making a Coherent America possible.

Although deliberately elicited by a process calling for relatively simple Big Ideas and fleshing these out in a logical manner, the discussion of the domestic-focused strategic concepts leads to an interesting interrelation among the three. Certainly, social cohesion and minimal polarization can make the prospect of achieving consensus on painful actions now, the better to improve outcomes in the long-term, more credible. Understanding the relationship among the strategic concepts and the implications of possible but currently unknown trends brings the discussion to the next step in applying the VSCARP method.

CHAPTER 3

Robust Pathways Toward Mid-Century

Strategic Concepts and Potential Future Outcomes

The strategic concepts detailed in Chapter 2 are all myopic to a degree—and by design. Although different in focus, they are also alternatives of each other. For some, the focus might be more domestic than global or vice versa. But they each offer a big answer to the big question of "What is to be done?" One strategy says that the United States needs to gain a sense of common domestic purpose. Another says the United States must understand the existential issues posed by a challenging China. Yet a third says the United States needs to arrange its economy and society so that basic human needs are addressed. Proponents of each would concede the importance of points raised about the other strategies. But all were generated from a perspective requiring their core insight to be dominant in how the United States builds its economy and society going forward. If not, they argue, then nothing else will really matter. Now begins the task of taking a more comprehensive view.

Figure 3.1 provides an integrated view of the five strategic concepts and the main themes that play a part in each. Although only an illustration, Figure 3.1 portrays how the emerging alternative strategies are no longer the simplistic bumper sticker strategic concepts elicited by the first part of the VSCARP methodology as an analytically useful place to begin. The further steps in the process yield greater insight into individual strategic concepts and the relationship among them. The next step brings these relationships more strongly to the fore.

In the workshop's prior small-group breakout sessions in which participants were asked to conceive of bumper sticker concepts for strategic alternatives, they were also asked to consider what key **assumptions** might be supporting each such concept. These assumptions were elaborated further in Step 5 along with consideration of which could prove vulnerable to future events or trends. VSCARP further applies assumption-based planning to consider where there might be important switch points between and within strategies in line with identified **signpost** indicators tied to those key assumption vulnerabilities (Step 6). Such signposts are indicators specially selected to provide early warning that the future, as it unfolds, could stress the assumptions underlying the original strategy to the extent that the intended long-term outcomes fail to be achieved. How might a particular strategy be made more robust to future uncertainties by introducing specific adaptive actions? When would it be possible and how could prior preparations make it feasible to hybridize strategies—that is, shift toward a course of action consistent with a more conducive strategic approach?

FIGURE 3.1
Consolidated Strategic Concepts and Their Selective Focus on Major Themes

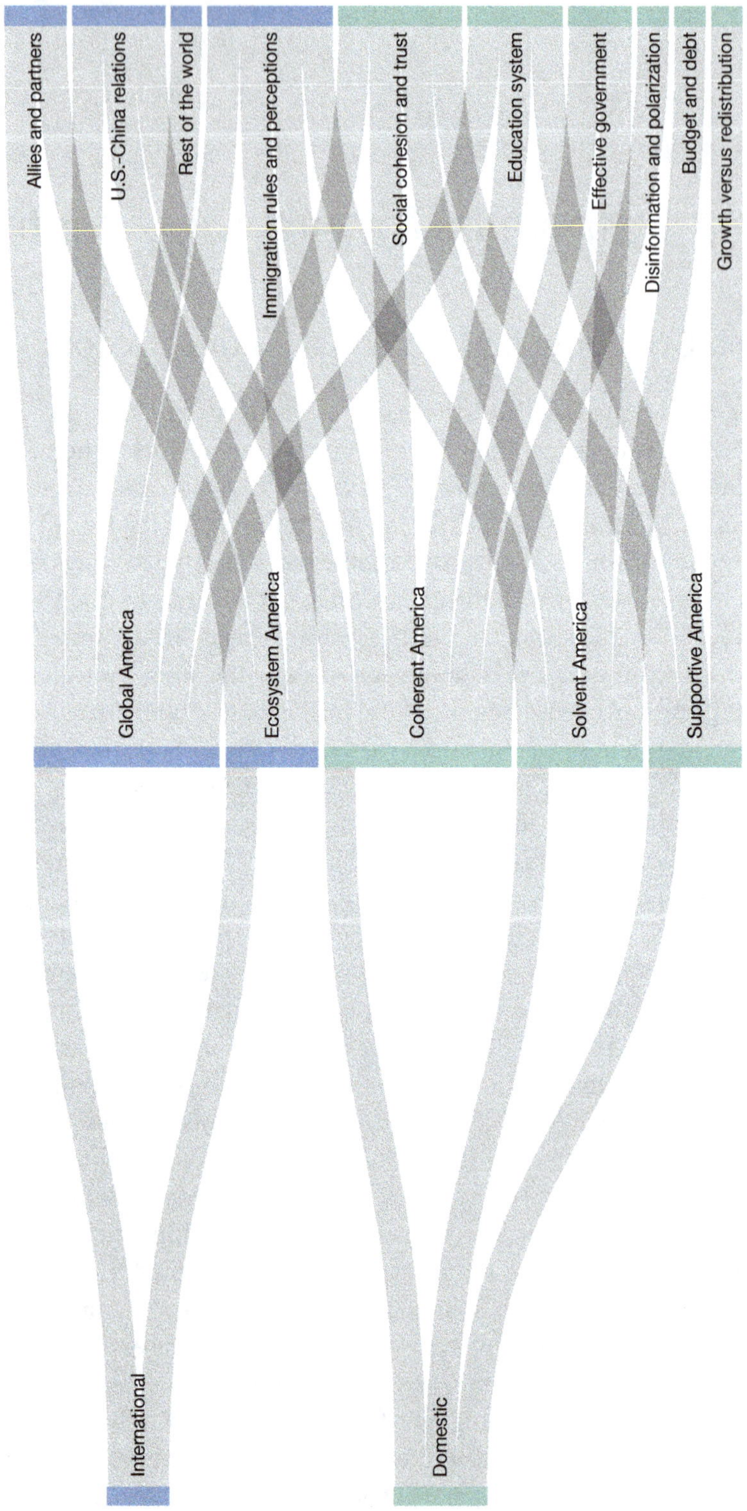

Having previously defined the characteristics of favorable and unfavorable future outcomes as framed by a consensus 2040 vision—and having identified the strategic concepts governing alternative pathways forward (along with their load-bearing assumptions)—participants were then placed in a plenary session to identify different scenarios of future outcomes (Step 7).[1] The scenarios were composed, in part, of four future end states for the U.S. economy of 2040. Using the criteria for the 2040 vision, the scenarios are as follows:

- **Flourishing.** The United States largely meets the expectations enshrined in the desiderata for the year 2040.
- **Holding Our Own.** The United States navigates a tough environment but at least approaches near fulfillment of most of the desiderata comprising the 2040 vision. The United States possesses economic power and international relationships to attract talent, access materials and markets, and maintain technological leadership in most of the globally important technical areas, as well as to exercise a meaningful degree of hard and soft power. Domestically, there is opportunity for U.S. citizens to prosper, the United States is an important player in the global sustainability effort, the domestic social safety net is secure, the middle class grows at least incrementally, and the U.S. academic community continues to be among world leaders.
- **Getting By.** The United States goes through tough sailing that involves compromises and trade-offs among the elements of the 2040 vision and therefore leads to less desirable outcomes. The United States manages to maintain parity with strategic competitors, and it keeps rogue nations, such as Iran and North Korea, at bay, but does so by having to work hard and expend resources to protect national interests. The domestic situation is more difficult than in Holding Our Own, but not to the extent that it causes either the United States' domestic or global position to decline substantially.
- **Not Making It.** The United States is largely not meeting the expectations for the U.S. economy in 2040.

It should be noted that Not Making It and, in several respects, Getting By, would represent loss of ground compared with the situation of the U.S. economy in 2024.

The second day began with further plenary discussion to determine what the assumptions were behind each of the five strategic concepts developed on the first day, which assumptions were truly key (in the sense that were they to be broken, one would no longer be able to recommend a strategic course predicated on those assumptions), and how such assumptions

---

[1] The term *scenario* is often somewhat loosely defined and applied. In many cases, the term has been connected to a static portrait of a particular future state of the world. Within the VSCARP methodology, a scenario embraces not only a set of possible future states of the world that share distinctive characteristics in common but also a narrative pathway leading to that future. This is a more restrictive use of the term in keeping with the original conception developed by Herman Kahn in the 1950s and 1960s. See, for example, Herman Kahn and Anthony J. Wiener, *The Year 2000: A Framework for Speculation on the Next Thirty-Three Years*, Macmillan, 1967.

might be vulnerable. Participants were invited to consider, for each strategy, what might be appropriate **hedging** or **shaping** actions associated with that strategy as the future unfolds. A *hedging action* is one that would stem the downside loss if the future turns out to be unfavorable to a strategy. (The classic hedging action is to take out an insurance policy). A *shaping action* is an active measure to bend the external environment toward conditions conducive to the strategy (advertising campaigns are examples of shaping actions). Identifying signposts and potential hedging and shaping actions to be employed depending on how events and trends proceed is a useful means for enhancing the robustness of any given strategy. It also provides valuable information for considering how strategies might be hybridized to build on their strengths and diminish their weaknesses. When considering a set of alternative strategies, cognizance of their respective actions, assumptions, and implications helps consideration of when to "get off the horse you are riding" and switch to another better-positioned strategy to carry into a future more likely to be resonant with the long-term vision.

These elements—assumptions, vulnerabilities, signposts, and hedging and shaping actions—were used to sketch out what pathways toward 2040 might look like for each strategic concept. Each strategic concept is briefly sketched in the following figures. The nodes along the various lines represent either branching points or important "way stations" that identify critical elements affecting the outcomes for each strategy.

Global America

Figure 3.2 shows selected major pathways emerging from following the Global America strategy. The figure begins in the present (on the left) and, depending on unfolding conditions and potential responses to them, could arrive at divergent outcomes by 2040 (on the right). The way stations and branch points indicated by the labeled dots are a synthesis of the workshop discussion of the interplay between key assumptions, their vulnerabilities and consequences, and possible hedging and shaping actions. (Appendix B provides a gazetteer spelling out the necessarily abbreviated labels used in Figures 3.2 through 3.7.)

For this strategy to result in a flourishing U.S. economy in 2040, a combination of strong international investment by the United States, allied support, international cooperation (including with China), and wise and effective domestic investment must occur as indicated by the upper line in the figure. In the absence of sufficiently strong domestic and international support ("Global minus" node in the figure), the future likely hinges on the outcome of cooperation and competition with China. Depending on the nature of the interaction and the constraints it places on the United States, the unfolding of the Global America strategy could follow the indicated pathways to the middle futures if trade agreements resolving difficulties come into place. In the worst case, heavy competition that favors China could cause the U.S. economy to fail to meet expectations.

FIGURE 3.2

Pathways for Global America Showing Major Signposts Associated with Vulnerabilities to Key Assumptions

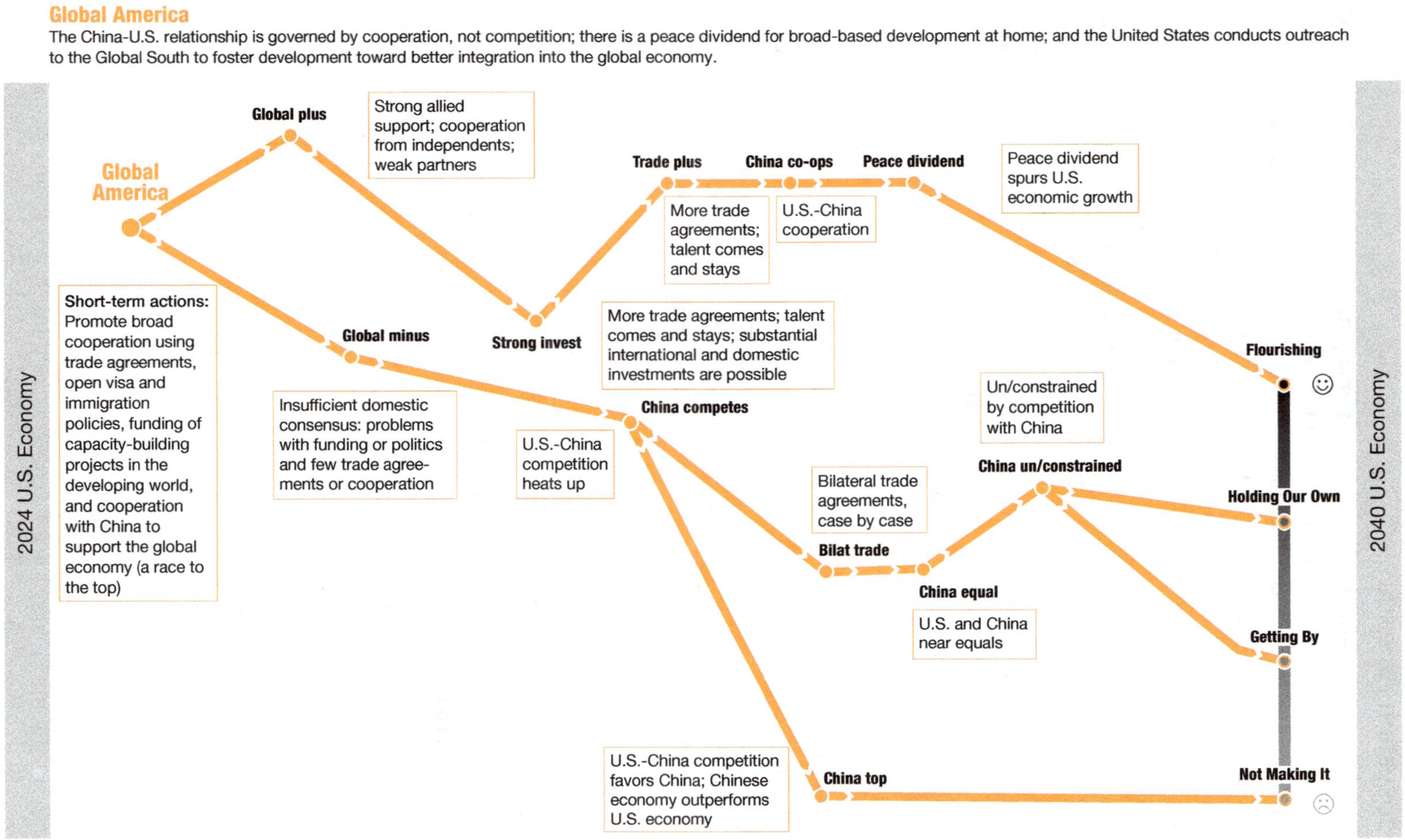

Ecosystem America

Figure 3.3 shows selected major pathways emerging from following the Ecosystem America strategy. Following this course would lead to a flourishing state of the U.S. economy in 2040 if there transpires a combination of strong U.S. investments and expanded international economic relationships that brings China into agreement to strengthen economic engagement with the United States. Failing the establishment of strong international economic relationships envisioned by proponents (the "Eco minus" node), the future likely hinges on the outcome of competition with China. An important factor will be whether there is strong across-the-board U.S. investment or, because of constraints, a more considered approach that focuses on the various arenas of strategic competition—economic and others—to the neglect of other needs. The strategy could follow pathways to the mid-range outcomes if such strategic U.S. investment and bilateral and multilateral trade agreements—and the result of U.S.-China competition—allow. In the worst case, China's economy outperforms that of the United States and the U.S. economy fails to meet expectations.

Solvent America

Figure 3.4 depicts major pathways that could ensue following the Solvent America strategy to 2040. The strategy is predicated on the assumption that there is a growing risk of unsustainable budget constraints moving toward mid-century. For this strategy to result in a flourishing U.S. economy, the United States must address its existing budgetary and financing difficulties and make substantial international and domestic investments that ensure a strong dollar, the desirability of the United States as a global partner, and the growth of the U.S. middle class. Were budget and financial difficulties to be relieved only partially (the "Solvent minus" node) or if there is policy unwillingness to strongly invest, strategic domestic and international investments could lead to the U.S. economy in Holding Our Own or Getting By statuses. The difference would once again be the indirect constraints imposed by competition with China and would only in part be determined by U.S. choices. Actual outcomes from U.S.-China competition would play a role as well. In the worst case, the United States cannot resolve its budget and financial problems, faces borrowing constraints, and cannot afford critical investments, and the U.S. economy fails to meet expectations.

FIGURE 3.3
Pathways for Ecosystem America Showing Major Signposts Associated with Vulnerabilities to Key Assumptions

Ecosystem America
The United States is the center of a mutually beneficial economic network; the United States attracts the global best and brightest; there is extensive domestic education, training, and skill development; U.S.-China competition is a race to the top, not the bottom; and there is a new economic NATO with members from TPP, TTIP, and MERCOSUR/L.

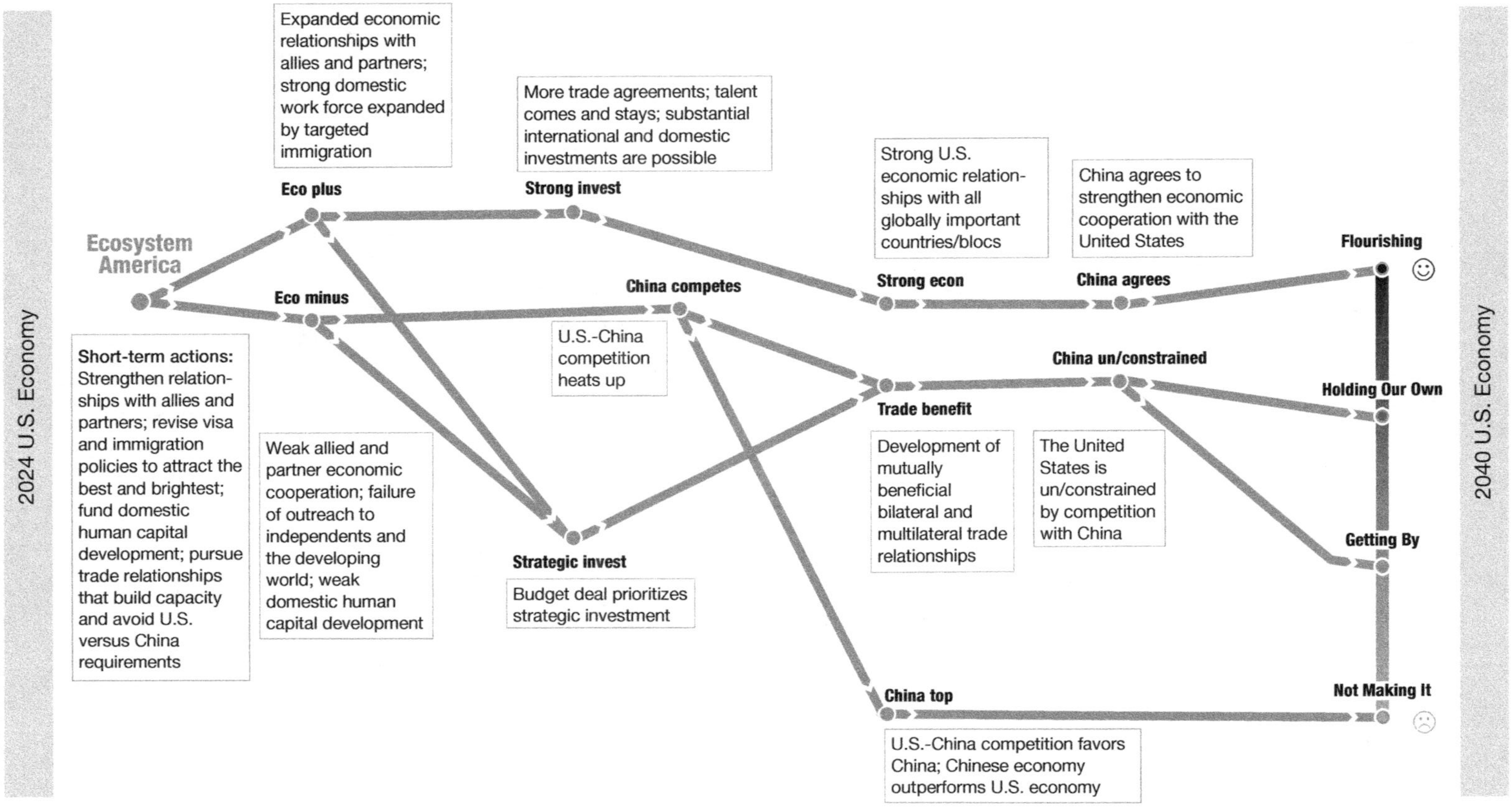

FIGURE 3.4

Pathways for Solvent America Showing Major Signposts Associated with Vulnerabilities to Key Assumptions

Solvent America

There is a digital dollar with smart contracts to yield transparency and accountability; there is fiscal sustainability and a strategic, prioritized budget that reflects the U.S. public's values and interests; and the U.S. government's budget process reflects existing realities.

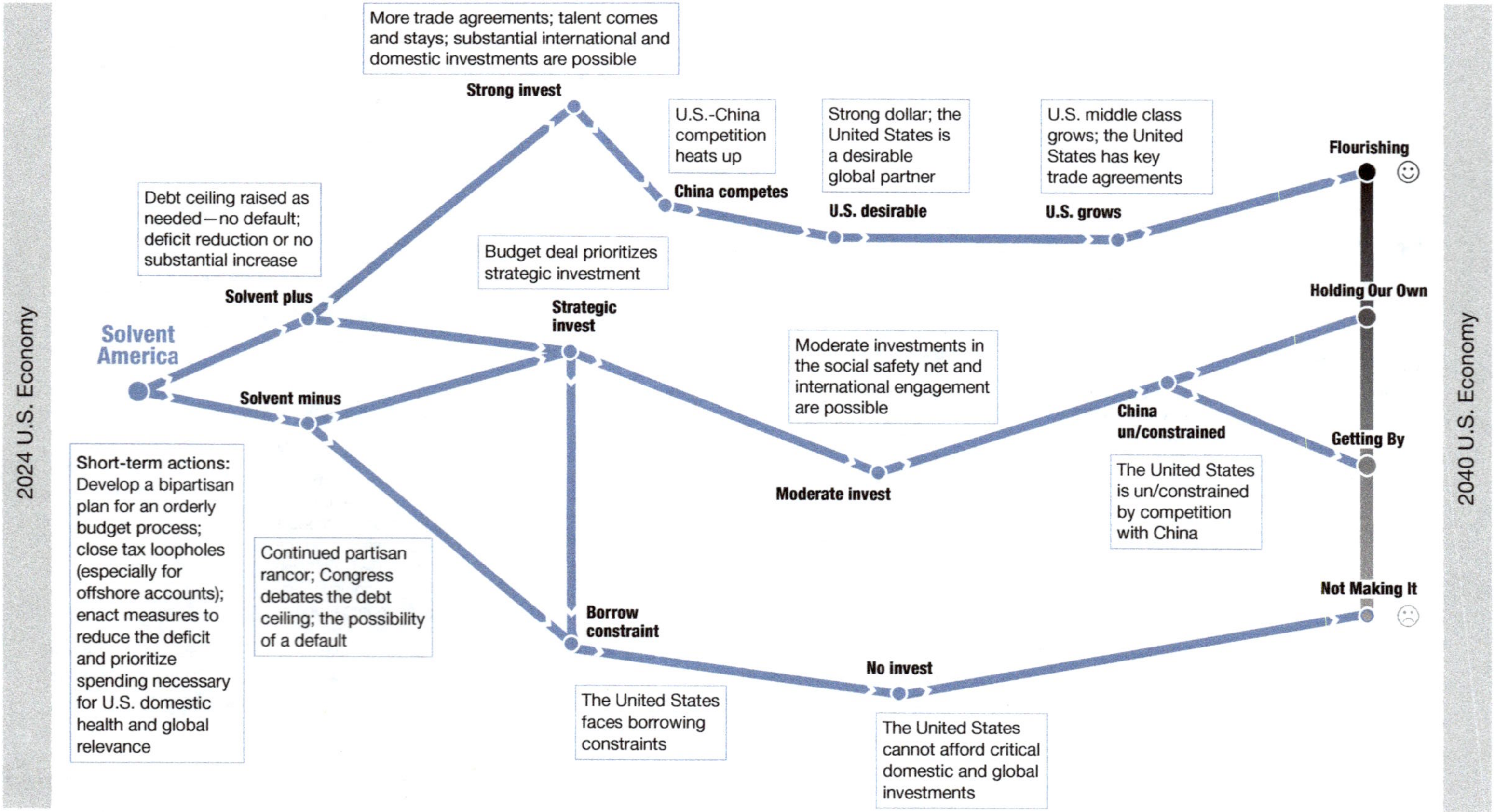

Supportive America

Figure 3.5 shows selected major pathways emerging from following Supportive America, a largely domestic-oriented strategy. For this strategy to result in a flourishing U.S. economy in 2040, the United States must make strong, well-planned, and well-executed domestic investments that result in improvements in the availability and quality of housing and health care and the growth of the middle class, which would result in increased social stability and well-being. Well-planned and -executed strategic investments could lead to either of the middle futures; the result would depend on how a bifurcated economy develops—one in which opportunity and a sense of well-being are perceived as being dependent on structural inequalities. The two different end states of Holding Our Own and Getting By would largely be determined by consequences that ensue from that perception. In the worst case, failure to provide sufficient investment for domestic needs leads to an economy that fails its citizens, a likelihood of lower quality and less availability of housing and health care, increased homelessness, and a potential for civil unrest. Although strategic competition with China does not formally appear in Figure 3.5, the indirect effects of such competition might be large and determine the available amounts of U.S. investment of resources and policy attention.

Coherent America

Pathways for the final strategy, Coherent America, are shown in Figure 3.6. For this strategy to result in a flourishing U.S. economy in 2040, government and private-sector actions to reduce the spread of misinformation and increase public faith in institutions must achieve success in reducing divisiveness and gaining wide support from the U.S. public. In particular, the public would need to support a strong investment in big projects that unify the country, result in shared prosperity, increase the size of the middle class, decrease social unrest, and increase social well-being. Failing this, a truce in partisan warfare coupled with strategic investment in projects to promote the public good could still lead to one of the middle futures (Holding Our Own or Getting By), depending on how many aspects of the nine desiderata for the U.S. economy (listed in Chapter 2) a splintered public and body politic can achieve. In the worst case, partisan conflict, loss of faith in a dysfunctional government, and civil unrest result in the U.S. economy failing to achieve most of the goals laid out in the vision for 2040.

FIGURE 3.5

Pathways for Supportive America Showing Major Signposts Associated with Vulnerabilities to Key Assumptions

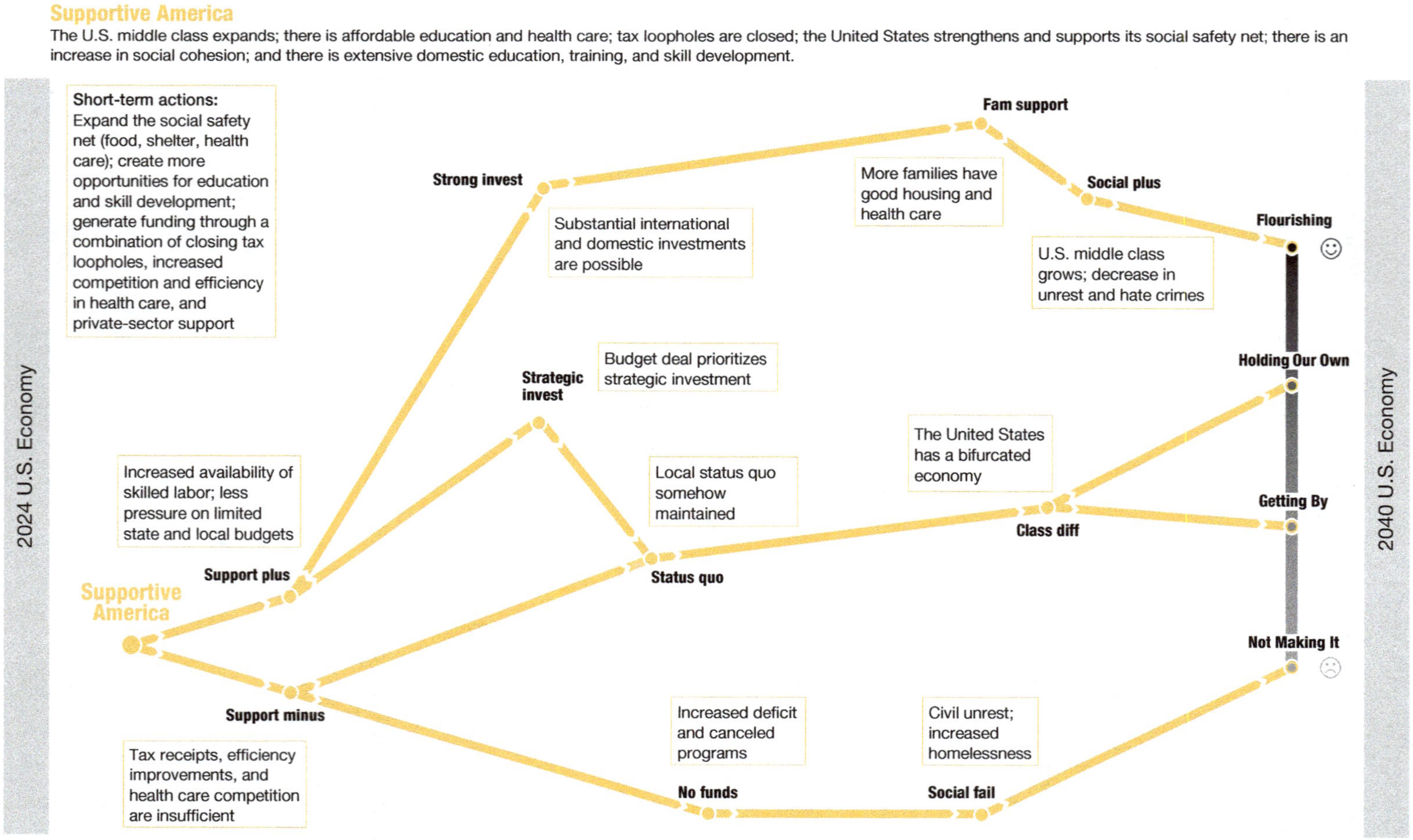

FIGURE 3.6

Pathways for Coherent America Showing Major Signposts Associated with Vulnerabilities to Key Assumptions

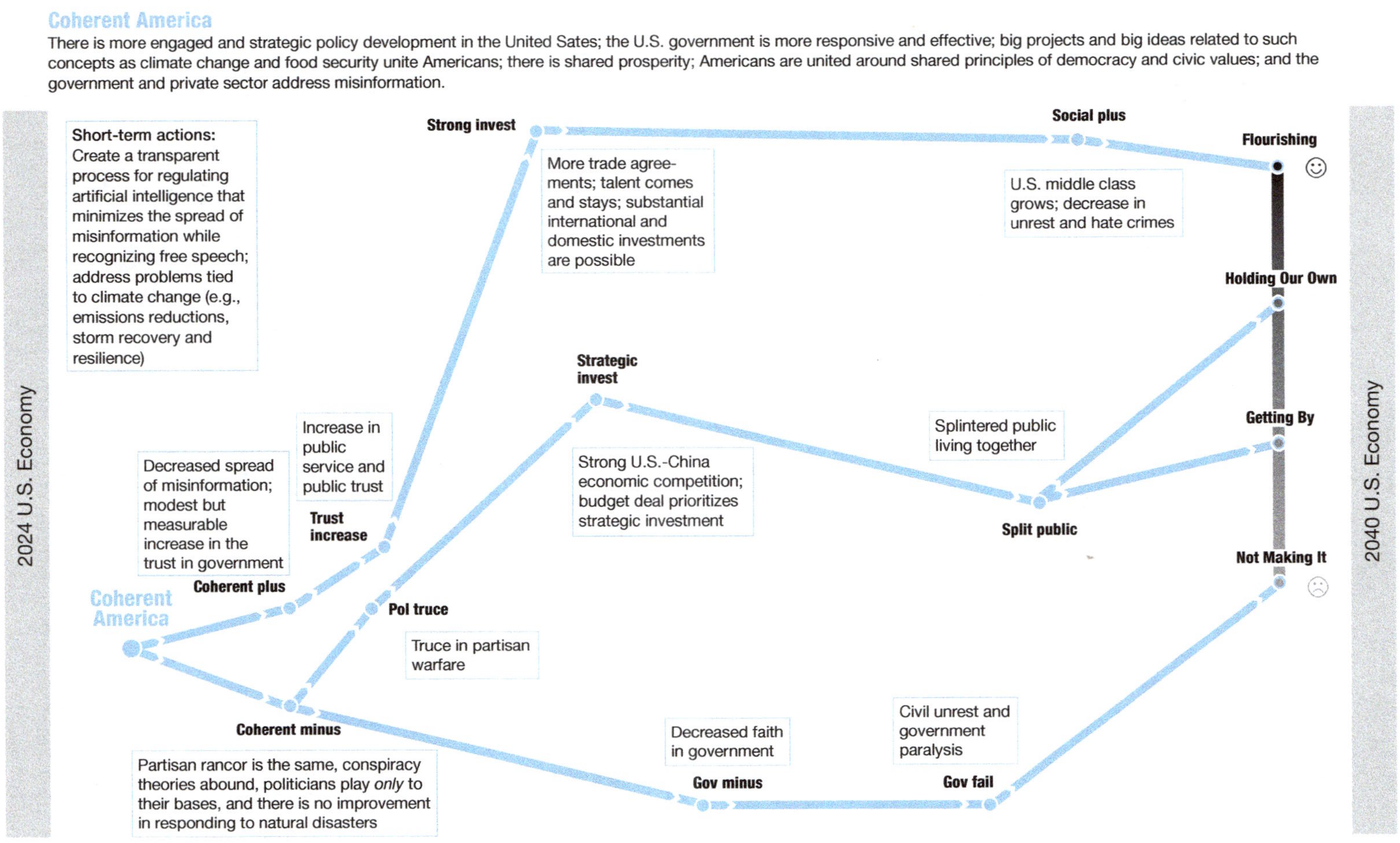

Alternative Pathways to 2040

In each of the five relatively narrow strategic concepts, there exists a theoretical pathway toward a flourishing U.S. economy in 2040. In each case, however, to reach this outcome, there is a need for full implementation of the tenets and actions spelled out for each strategy—as well as some good fortune in how the world responds to those actions. Each strategy is fragile to potential vulnerable assumptions, some of which face entirely plausible threats. Any one selected strategy could therefore well prove to be brittle to trends or events as the future unfolds. Although initially presented as distinct alternatives for the purpose of elaboration and discussion, it is now possible to consider the relationship among them.

As a practical matter, any statement of an operational course of action would need to consider how to draw in important elements of each of the five idealized strategic concepts and the courses of actions they imply. Furthermore, there is no need to presume and perhaps even less likelihood to expect that policy persistence across U.S. presidential administrations would be so strong as to see a resulting hybridized strategy, no matter how well-constructed, pursued unflinchingly across several decades. If nothing else, a robust approach requires that there be off-ramps from a strategic course that might find conditions stressful to the vulnerable assumptions on which they are based, be they domestic or foreign.

Figure 3.7 is an amalgamation of the five strategies' charted pathways. It is presented in a manner similar to a map of a public transit system. The way stations are the main features revealed by the assumption-based planning discussion of load-bearing assumptions, potential vulnerabilities, and early-warning signpost indicators and were represented in Figures 3.2 through 3.6. These way stations have been abbreviated for convenience in Figure 3.7. A gazetteer showing what the abbreviations correspond to is in Appendix B.

There is no implied order to the vertical alignment of the points from which the pathways commence in 2024 (the left side in Figure 3.7). Their arrangement from top to bottom is intended to best display how they interconnect at important junctions across time. There is, however, order to where they conclude on the right-hand side in 2040. The outcomes from top to bottom are in descending order of perceived success according to the 2040 vision criteria for the United States. At several points, pathways appear to terminate short of 2040, but they should be understood as continuing along the same line as shown to the same endpoint.[2]

Overlaying the five pathways for each strategic concept on top of each other helps reveal several insights. All four future states for the U.S. economy in 2040 are, in theory, reachable by any of the five strategies that begin in 2023. Not all pathways, however, are equal to the extent in which their underlying assumptions might come into serious question. That is, what assumptions one would need to believe will hold true in the future to recommend the course of action associated with the strategy might be harder to credit than for other alternative

[2] These instances should be interpreted as showing that a particular pathway ensuing from one strategy created the conditions at the point of intersection that enable another strategy to proceed along the shared pathway.

FIGURE 3.7
Five Strategic Pathways for the 2040 U.S. Economy Showing Potential Challenges and Branch Points

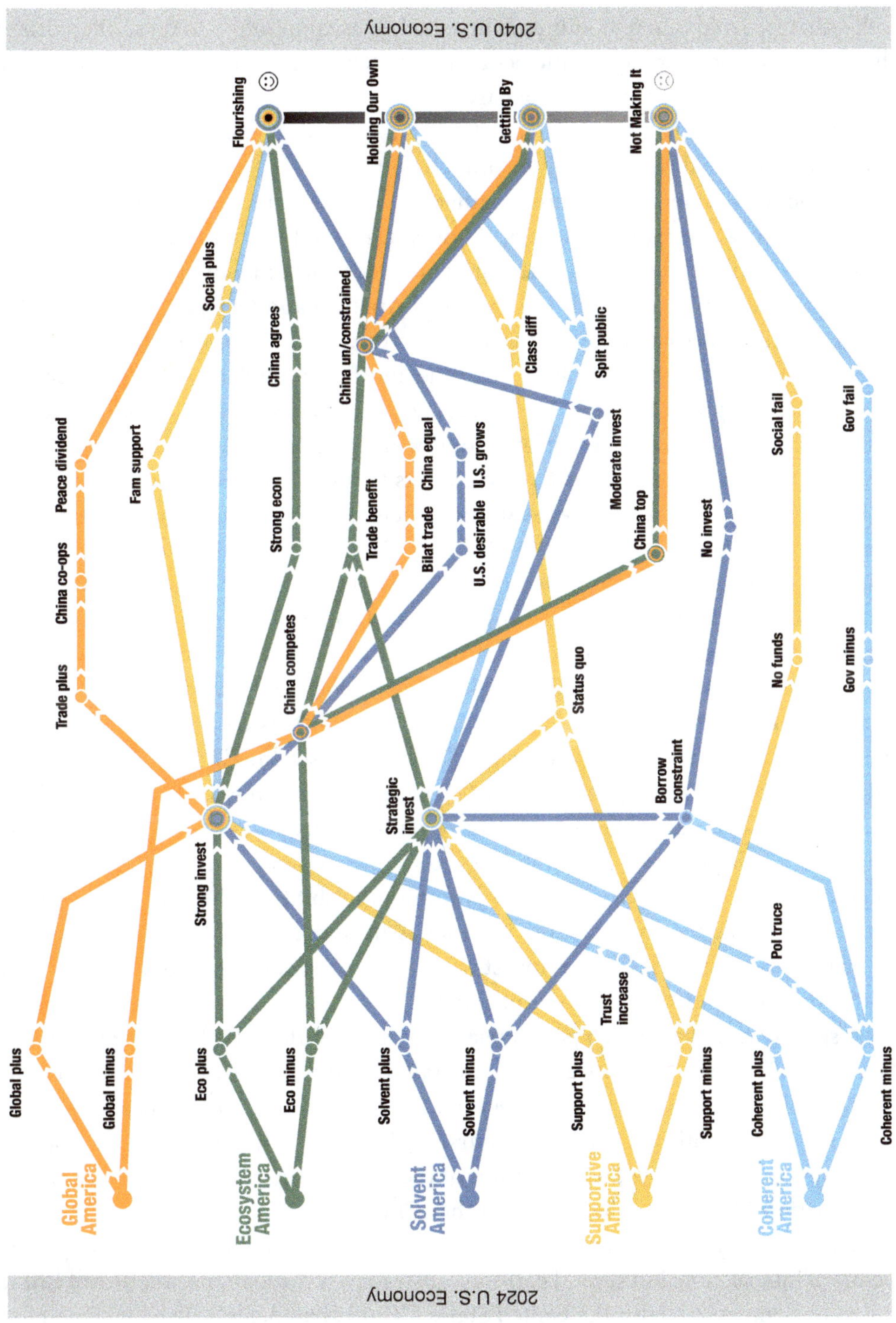

courses of actions depending on that or other strategies. Although all pathways can lead to flourishing in 2040, some of the strategies might need a larger share of trends or events to go well—that is, avoid inherent vulnerabilities to key assumptions—to do so than others. What the figure does not portray are the hedging and shaping actions associated with each branch point. These actions would become part of an operational plan that would seek to navigate pathways toward higher-placed 2040 outcomes for a strategy confronted with a potential vulnerability associated with each of the branch points.

The points of intersection across pathways are of the greatest interest in this figure and bring into focus several key findings. Although having been formed and then presented as formal alternatives, the group of strategies is in fact related in complicated ways. Some may be seen as alternatives (most clearly in Global America and Ecosystem America; the former requires active engagement by China as a predicate), but they could more properly be considered as elements that could bootstrap one another in implementation if placed within a composite strategic framework. The more lines that intersect at a single point, the greater the concern for how the transition at that point will frame the trajectories of the pathways that have entered. From this perspective, the points that occur earliest are those that are rooted in U.S. budgetary issues and the resulting capacity for investment in national priorities. The points "Strong invest," "Strategic invest," and "Borrow constraint" form a triad. They correspond, respectively, to situations in which the United States is able to invest widely and deeply, needs to be more strategic and selective in its spending priorities, or faces serious constraints in doing even that.

Looking at the branch points that lie along various pathways immediately prior to (to the left of) each of these common nodes, we find conditions determined in part by issues of public trust ("Trust increase"), solvency ("Solvent plus/minus"), and being able to develop sufficiently broad political consensus ("Coherent plus/minus"; "Pol truce"). The branch points marked plus and minus emanating from the start point of each strategy relate to the extent to which perceived vulnerabilities to the key assumptions underlying each strategy might actually come to pass and so compromise the ability of the strategy to meet intended objectives. As the figure shows, the solvency issue and availability of investment resources, along with the will to make those investments, appears crucial beyond the narrow purview of the Solvent America strategic concept alone.

A second set of key switch points relates to the evolution of relations between the United States and China and the stance that China takes. This is largely owing to the pressure placed on available resources and policy attention. A China finding, on balance, value in reaching accommodation with U.S. actions in pursuit of its own interests ("China co-ops") is a key stepping stone to achieve the realization of the Global America strategy in its most hopeful instantiation. This is also the essence of the "China agrees" way station along the Ecosystem America pathway. Both, however, are situations that occur along single pathways and are not points of intersection. But several pathways instead pass through the juncture of China choosing to be competitive with the United States ("China competes"). The outcome of that contest, in turn, determines how the U.S. strategies fare. These relations have indirect influence on eventual outcomes depending on the United States' ability to apply constraints ("China un/constrained"), achieve and maintain at least a condition of parity ("China equal"), or deal with the consequences of confronting an able competitor ("China top").

A more detailed examination of the figure could suggest important tipping points for either hybridizing strategies or determining when it might be best to shift to a different course of action from an implementation depending on one strategic course to that of an alternative. That detailed analysis would be part of a subsequent analytical process and so require a level of detail that will not be pursued in this report; however, Figure 3.7 suggests how such maneuvering could be most effective.[3] A hybridization approach could be pursued by deliberating on the perceived vulnerabilities to key assumptions and their associated signposts generated by the assumption-based planning component of VSCARP. That is, elements of two or more strategies might be accommodated as part of a re-tooled strategic concept to enhance its robustness in implementation. By including elements from a different strategic concept that might, in fact, be better suited to circumstances assessed as potentially giving rise to stressful futures for an original strategic concept, the vulnerability to several plausible deleterious scenarios might be reduced—and, with it, the potential for unacceptable outcomes. It is clear, for example, that no amalgamation of the strategic concepts would be well-advised to ignore including aspects of the Solvent America concept as part of its fully fleshed out strategic guidance.

Hedging and Shaping Actions

Figure 3.7, with its "plus" and "minus" nodes, provides the signposts for identifying when hedging and shaping actions and strategic hybridization might be necessary. These actions would be employed from the pathways' onset and during the entire course. For example, were the strong international cooperation associated with the "Global plus" node to emerge from pursuing the Global America strategy, investment in increasing global outreach, diplomacy, and trade agreements would be promising shaping actions. Similarly, were weak economic cooperation and failed outreach associated with the "Eco minus" node to result from pursuing the Ecosystem America strategy, limited strategic investment aimed at maintaining the United States's global economic importance in the face of competition with China could be an effective hedging option.

With respect to the domestic strategies, if the conditions described in "Support plus" or "Coherent plus" were to ensue as a result of pursuing the Supportive America or Coherent America strategies, investment in social programs and federal government support of national priorities would be shaping actions. The conditions in "Support minus" or "Coherent minus"

[3] Ideally, the original workshop participants and new entrants to widen the pool would be presented with output similar to that presented in Chapter 3 for further deliberation and reconsideration. Many of the same techniques employed in VSCARP would be iterated using this new input to provide greater detail and begin to hybridize the relatively simple original strategic concepts.

would highlight the importance of hedging actions and policies, such as limited prioritized investments aimed at maintaining current levels of societal well-being and social cohesion.

As noted in the previous section, Figure 3.7 indicates that the level of investment that is possible in domestic and international initiatives will determine the United States' flexibility to respond to evolving conditions with shaping and hedging actions. That flexibility will, in turn, be determined by the success or lack of success in solving the U.S. government's financial solvency problems; i.e., pursuit of the Solvent America strategy might result in continued partisan rancor and potential default ("Solvent minus") or agreement on a stable and sustainable budget process ("Solvent plus").

The hedging and shaping actions described previously are based on conditions that result from pursuit of the five strategies in the near term. As the envisioned scenario pathways evolve and load-bearing assumptions either come to pass or fail, available transition points, analogous to transfer stations in a public transit system, become more limited and more difficult to craft. However, unlike with public transit transfer stations, there is not necessarily any way back to the beginning because some aspects of future conditions might already be set. In that situation, Figure 3.7 provides a means for planning shaping and hedging initiatives to be executed under more-challenging circumstances at a later time.

Toward Robust Action Plans

Findings from the workshop to this point constitute not so much conclusions as a beginning—a common basis for more-detailed elaborations, planning, and implementation. The discussion during the final plenary session was a first step in that direction.

Participants explored what a robust approach for achieving many of the elements of the 2040 vision might look like. A robust plan is one that is designed to achieve defined, measurable levels of successful outcomes across a variety of possible future conditions. A robust plan includes (1) an agreed set of short-term, low-regret actions,[4] (2) a set of optional actions that may or may not be employed in the medium term, and (3) criteria for judging the need and appropriateness of each medium-term action.

Using the results of the prior two days, the suggested short-term actions reflected two principal concerns:

- China can best be managed through a slow, deliberate approach that looks for reciprocal signals and actions. This can be enhanced by broadening the remit of bilateral relations

[4] *Regret* is a concept for comparing alternatives. Low regret does not guarantee success; under some conditions, none of the available alternatives will succeed. Regret is measured as what we would lose by choosing one action compared with its alternatives. At least one option would be deemed the zero-regret choice because none of the other options would achieve more (or lose less) under stipulated future conditions. In the absence of credible prediction, the task is to determine which alternative to choose. When many alternative strategies are considered, low-regret actions are those found as constituent elements of many or most strategies that see successful outcomes.

with other partners in the Indo-Pacific region and expanding existing institutions to include more countries. This was judged as low regret both because of the ability to tune deterrence to appropriate levels and because such measures are usually not of a profile to stir partisan domestic concerns.

- A bipartisan commission on issues related to fiscal affairs could take a hard look at the budget process but also at the incentives for politicians to recommit to a responsibility for governance and stewardship of governmental outcomes. This would be low regret and a potential signal indicating whether some of the mapped pathways could be realized or instead require strategic rethinking. In any case, traditional budget processes do not seem to fit in the United States of the 21st century. Several specific changes were offered, but the general agreement was on the need for reframing the process in the context of both constitutional authorities and the realities of the modern age.

CHAPTER 4

Reflections and Considerations

> The conflict as it concerns the democracy to which our history commits us is *within* our own institutions and attitudes. It can be won only by extending the application of democratic methods, methods of consultation, persuasion, negotiation, communication, co-operative intelligence, in the task of making our own politics, industry, education, our cultures generally, a servant and an evolving manifestation of democratic ideas. . . . [D]emocratic ends demand democratic methods for their realization. . . . An American democracy can serve the world only as it demonstrates in the conduct of its own life the efficacy of plural, partial, and experimental methods in securing and maintaining an ever-increasing release of the powers of human nature, in service of a freedom which is co-operative and a co-operation which is voluntary.
>
> —*Freedom and Culture*, John Dewey (1939), pp. 175–176

A core tenet of the Defense Advanced Research Projects Agency, the sponsor of this research, is to be disruptive not necessarily by making something but rather in demonstrating that something can be made. The research activity that this report highlights was conducted in that spirit. It was an effort to engineer an apparatus for bringing disparate individuals and groups together to perform difficult tasks under considerable uncertainty without the need for any participant to abdicate core beliefs and tenets.

The exercise we report on was carried out at a small scale, with compressed timing, and with necessarily limited participation. It concluded at the intended endpoint, illustrated in Figure 3.7, as part of the initial exploratory effort of this research. A next step, of course, would be to return to the original group of participants, augmented by a wider circle of participants, to validate and modify these findings. The participants would then proceed along the next step to consider how the five relatively simple strategies could be hybridized into a more nuanced and more robust strategy toward building the mid-century U.S. economy. The foundation built during the actual workshops is too narrow to make firm recommendations or establish unassailable guidelines. Nevertheless, several themes emerged that appear reasonable enough to suppose a wider, broader, and more intense effort using the same approach would endorse them. The themes are as follows:

- **Vision.** There are important elements of a vison for a desirable mid-century U.S. economy that can receive endorsement from individuals and across groups possessing different interests, perceptions, worldviews, and sets of assumptions.

- **Obstacles and opportunities.** Domestic policies and actions can enable movement toward or provide barriers to reaching desirable U.S. economic futures. This reinforces a sense of agency in the realm of federal policy making that has sometimes been obscured in recent years.
- **Forks in the road.** Important nodes that affect trajectories along several defined pathways include
  - the future U.S. capacity for investment, both foreign and domestic
  - the need to plan and provide political framing for, consensus on, and defined strategic goals of such investment
  - effective management of the relationship with China for the benefit of both countries and the globe—an outcome not determined solely by U.S. actions.
- **External relations.** Strong relationships with allies and outreach to developing countries that is not primarily couched in terms of the U.S.-China strategic competition can support movement toward desirable U.S. economic futures.

Taken together, these themes provide a coherent message: a future U.S. economy that achieves all or most of the desiderata described in Chapter 1 will likely require successfully linking targeted domestic and security-oriented investment with international relationships of mutual benefit.

Several key process (as opposed to product) outcomes emerged that suggest the potential for further deliberations in which the VSCARP approach can be employed at a larger scale of engagement and with a greater capacity for deliberation and meaningful multiparty interaction:

- **Complexities made observable.** It is possible to elaborate complex relationships across time, policy domains, and categories of interest and share them in a manner designed to enhance a collective ability to observe them.
- **Structure for dynamic deliberation.** A systematic, structured process can enable groups of individuals with highly varied training and expertise to think dynamically across an evolving domestic and international landscape in which each successive period possesses changing requirements for success.
- **Assumptions and strategic alternatives.** A process exists for sharing alternative strategic concepts; examining them simultaneously for key assumptions, vulnerabilities, and performance outcomes; and, moreover, identifying for each strategy signpost indicators for monitoring, shaping strategies to enhance the prospects for success, and hedging actions to limit downside risks.
- **Deliberation with analysis.** Participatory foresight can provide an important element within a larger framing to provide deliberation with analysis as the leading edge of a more detailed integration of policy deliberation with analytical decision support.[1]

[1] The National Research Council has characterized an iterative process of "deliberation with analysis" as the best approach to deliberating what it calls "wicked" problems (Paul C. Stern and Harvey V. Fineberg, eds., *Understanding Risk: Informing Decisions in a Democratic Society*, National Academy Press, 1996).

The VSCARP method was applied to a problem statement that was very general in scope. Its application was sufficient as a relatively rapid standalone process to engage interest from different types of professionals, provide them with a sense of having received value in exchange for their participation, and identify important elements for consideration and lay out the often complex causal links between them. VSCARP can be brought to bear on similar wide-ranging issues or on more-targeted areas in which policy is obscured by prevailing deep uncertainties. In addition, the method lends itself to setting up one of several follow-on efforts delving more deeply into questions raised, vulnerabilities exposed, and opportunities and pathways disclosed. Such an effort could bring to bear more-quantitative tools—including models, data mining, and the methods emerging from the developing field of decisionmaking under deep uncertainty.[2]

---

[2] The design for how a more detailed, model-based effort could follow and be integrated with a VSCARP process for advanced policy deliberation with analytical support may be found in Steven W. Popper, "Designing a Robust Decision–Based National Security Policy Process: Strategic Choices for Uncertain Times," in Aaron B. Frank and Elizabeth M. Bartels, eds., *Adaptive Engagement for Undergoverned Spaces: Concepts, Challenges, and Prospects for New Approaches*, RAND Corporation, RR-A1275-1, 2022.

APPENDIX A

Workshop Overview and Participants

We drew from an extended series of workshops that were conducted in two phases.

Workshop 1

The first workshop in the series was conducted by RAND and included RAND employees. The intent was to gain background from RAND experts on evolving U.S. relationships with other countries: allies, partners, potential adversaries, and other states important to U.S. interests. Any U.S. actions to preserve and enhance a competitive economy for itself by 2040 must play out across a web of geopolitical interactions and must be framed within this perspective to achieve the intended policy objectives. Therefore, the workshop focused on how countries and the country typologies that they and similar states fall into might react to U.S. actions—whether favorably or unfavorably—and what their responses might be.

The participants in Workshop 1 were all RAND associates, either staff or adjunct. They are listed in alphabetical order by last name and with their areas of regional focus in Table A.1.

The workshop included a mix of sessions to drill down on key issues and allow the full group to validate and build on perspectives from breakout groups as they reported their outcomes. The workshop began with six breakout groups consisting of three participants each. Each breakout group had a different assignment with participants representing one of the following groups:

- Group 1: Strongly tied U.S. partners not in Asia (e.g., Canada, the European Union, Mexico, the United Kingdom)
- Group 2: Strongly tied U.S. partners in Asia (e.g., Australia, Japan, South Korea)
- Group 3: Weakly tied U.S. partners (e.g., Colombia, Egypt, Nigeria, Thailand, Vietnam)
- Group 4: Major independent countries (e.g., Brazil, India, Indonesia, Saudi Arabia, South Africa, United Arab Emirates)
- Group 5: China and its allies and close partners
- Group 6: Russia and its allies and close partners.

The results from all six breakout group discussions were provided to a new set of three breakout groups of six participants. Each new larger group of six included one participant from each original country-type group. These second breakout groups then reviewed and discussed

TABLE A.1

Participants in Workshop 1 with Their Geographic Focuses and Workshop Group Assignments

Participants	Focus	Group
Naoko Aoki	Japan and East Asia	2
Cortez Cooper	China	5
William Courtney	Russia and former Soviet Union states	6
Alexis Dale-Huang	Korea, China	2
Rafiq Dossani	South Asia	4
Daniel Egel	Middle East	4
Edward Geist	Europe, Russia	6
Derek Grossman	Indo-Pacific region	5
Timothy Heath	China	5
Jeffrey Hornung	Japan	2
Marta Kepe	Western Europe, Baltics	1
Raymond Kuo	East Asia, Middle East	5
Jennifer Moroney	Australia, Southeast Asia	1
Alexander Noyes	Africa	3
Shona Olalere	Africa	3
Stephanie Pezard	Europe	1
Javier Rojas Aguilera	Latin America	3
Scott Savitz	Middle East	4
Elina Treyger	Russia and former Soviet Union states	6

NOTE: Group assignments are as follows: 1 = strongly tied U.S. partners not in Asia, 2 = strongly tied U.S. partners in Asia, 3 = weakly tied U.S. partners, 4 = major independent countries, 5 = China and its allies and close partners, 6 = Russia and its allies and close partners.

the constraints to the United States reaching a desirable 2040 future. The findings of the three latter groups were finally discussed and compiled in a plenary. The findings detailed how countries around the world might react to U.S. policies, especially the edge cases in which the benefits of cooperation were not obvious. The workshop highlighted that the main lens through which other countries would act would be their determination of their own national interest and how cooperation with or opposition to the United States—even when costly—would benefit them, especially if lack of cooperation or lack of opposition would be even more costly.

A highly condensed list of findings was prepared for the second workshop and reviewed to assist in informing the analysis prepared for this report.

Workshop 2

The principal findings in this report were derived from a second, two-day workshop held in person at the RAND office in Arlington, Virginia, on June 23–24, 2023.

This workshop had a mix of sessions that were not necessarily designed to arrive at detailed conclusions (to say nothing of consensus) by the end of two days. The workshop was instead designed to generate insights and elicit discussion that might then provide material for building a future in which the United States engages in fruitful economic relationships with its partners as well as other states, even potential strategic adversaries, within a framework that helps move the United States toward an explicit vision for the mid-century U.S. economy.

The workshop entailed a suite of methodologies tuned for group interaction and were designed to move forward a structured conversation. These included an integrated application of Three Horizon Foresight,[1] assumption-based planning,[2] backcasting,[3] and scenario generation.[4]

The goal of the first day was to provide a solid footing for an emerging vision by developing a rich understanding of what systems and forces make the vision sustainable in the future. Participants were enabled to identify where there are trade-offs between competing goals and where different stakeholder and community interests might lie.

A second phase entailed having participants raise and consider alternative pathways to reaching the 2040 vision. Scenarios were used not as ends in themselves but rather to map various trajectories toward implementation, to understand

- underlying assumptions and whether any of those assumptions might prove vulnerable to future events
- what effects might emerge during the course of implementing different strategies
- what signals would provide early warning that conditions not conducive to U.S. policies are developing
- what switch points might exist that would allow the United States to shift to other plans if obstacles or new opportunities emerge.

---

[1] See, for example, Andrew Curry and Anthony Hodgson, "Seeing in Multiple Horizons: Connecting Futures to Strategy," *Journal of Futures Studies*, Vol. 13, No. 1, August 2008.

[2] James A. Dewar, *Assumption-Based Planning: A Tool for Reducing Avoidable Surprises*, Cambridge University Press, 2002.

[3] Backcasting has been used widely in foresight studies, as described in Luke Georghiou, Jennifer Cassingena Harper, Michael Keenan, Ian Miles, and Rafael Popper, eds., *The Handbook of Technology Foresight: Concepts and Practice*, Edward Elgar, 2008.

[4] See, for example, Jerome C. Glenn and the Futures Group International, "Scenarios," in Jerome C. Glenn and Theodore J. Gordon, eds., *Futures Research Methodology—Version 3.0*, The Millennium Project, 2009; and Theodore J. Gordon, "Interactive Scenarios," in Jerome C. Glenn and Theodore J. Gordon, eds., *Futures Research Methodology—Version 3.0*, The Millennium Project, 2009.

The goal was not to solve the planning problem itself but instead to use a dynamic approach to better characterize a sustainable vision for a resilient U.S. economy in 2040.

Thus, the first day focused on developing visions of alternative futures, what might render the futures sustainable, and what near-term U.S. strategies, policies, and actions might support movement toward more-desirable futures. On the second day, participants then considered the constraints, conflicts, and trade-offs involved in pursuing the strategies from the first day and analyzed possible pathways from the present to 2040.

Participants in the workshop were solicited to include a wide span of backgrounds, interests, and perspectives. The resulting attendees were from wide-ranging backgrounds but the group was by no means comprehensive nor necessarily balanced. A larger effort would be required to achieve those ends.

The participants in Workshop 2 who attended both days and who agreed to be listed in this report are shown in alphabetical order by last name in Table A.2.

TABLE A.2

Workshop 2 Participants and Their Affiliations

Participant	Affiliation
Jake Chapman	Marque Ventures
Keith Crane	Science and Technology Policy Institute, Institute for Defense Analyses
Annie Do	Export-Import Bank of the United States
Daniel Drezner	Fletcher School, Tufts University
Eric French	University of Cambridge
Jason Galui	Cox School of Business, Southern Methodist University
Frank Liddy	RAND and Terranet Ventures
Maya MacGuineas	Committee for a Responsible Federal Budget
King Mallory	RAND
Christine McDaniel	Mercatus Center, George Mason University
Jonathan Moyer	Frederick S. Pardee Institute for International Futures, Denver University
Hilton Root	Schar School of Policy and Government, George Mason University
Howard Shatz	RAND

APPENDIX B

Gazetteer to the Way Stations Along the Strategic Concept Pathways to 2040

Figures 3.2–3.6 in the body of this report charted out pathways for five alternative strategies for moving from the present to a desirable future for the United States economy at mid-century. Those pathways and the nodes through which they pass were derived from workshop discussions that included framing strategic concepts, determining their underlying key assumptions, and considering how those assumptions might be vulnerable to future events and trends. In addition, participants considered what might be important signposts for each strategy—that is, early-warning signals that the future was taking a course either supportive of or inimical to the actions used in pursuit of the strategy.

This report does not present these findings in detail. Doing so would entail more pages than the average reader would likely sit still for. There is also a question of how much weight to put on a set of deliberations that were intended to be more illustrative than comprehensive. The five figures, along with a composite view in Figure 3.7, provide a shorthand for the main points raised during the workshop process. The practicalities of presentation necessitated a shorthand approach to labeling the nodes that describe the different pathways that each strategic course could follow. The gazetteer in Table B.1 is intended to be an aid to the reader in deciphering, in a bit more detail, what constitute the main elements surrounding each such node.

TABLE B.1
Way Stations Along the Strategic Concept Pathways to 2040: Shorthand and Descriptions

Node Shorthand	Node Description
Bilat trade	Multilateral agreement; shared cost
Borrow constraint	The United States faces borrowing constraints
China agrees	China agrees to strengthen economic cooperation with the United States
China competes	U.S.-China competition heats up
China co-ops	U.S.-China cooperation
China equal	The United States and China are near-equal competitors

Table B.1—Continued

Node Shorthand	Node Description
China top	U.S.-China competition favors China; Chinese economy outperforms U.S. economy
China un/constrained	The United States is un/constrained by competition with China
Class diff	The United States has a bifurcated economy
Coherent minus	Partisan rancor is the same, conspiracy theories abound, politicians play *only* to their bases, and there is no improvement in responding to natural disasters
Coherent plus	Decreased spread of misinformation; modest but measurable increase in the trust in government
Eco minus	Weak allied and partner economic cooperation; failure of outreach to independents and the developing world; weak domestic human capital development
Eco plus	Expanded economic relationships with allies and partners; strong domestic workforce expanded by targeted immigration
Fam support	More families have good housing and health care
Global minus	Insufficient domestic consensus: problems with funding or politics and few trade agreements or cooperation
Global plus	Strong allied support; cooperation from independents; weak partners
Gov fail	Civil unrest and government paralysis
Gov minus	Decreased faith in government
Moderate invest	Moderate investments in the social safety net and international engagement are possible
No funds	Increased deficit and canceled programs
No invest	The United States cannot afford critical domestic and global investments
Peace dividend	Peace dividend spurs U.S. economic growth
Pol truce	Truce in partisan warfare
Social fail	Civil unrest; increased homelessness
Social plus	U.S. middle class grows; decrease in unrest and hate crimes
Solvent minus	Continued partisan rancor; Congress debates the debt ceiling; the possibility of a default
Solvent plus	Debt ceiling raised as needed—no default; deficit reduction or no substantial increase
Split public	Splintered public living together

Table B.1—Continued

Node Shorthand	Node Description
Status quo	Local status quo somehow maintained
Strategic invest	Budget deal prioritizes strategic investment
Strong econ	Strong U.S. economic relationships with all globally important countries and blocs
Strong invest	More trade agreements; talent comes and stays; substantial international and domestic investments are possible
Support minus	Tax receipts, efficiency improvements, and competition in health care are insufficient
Support plus	Increased availability of skilled labor; less pressure on limited state and local budgets
Trade benefit	Development of mutually beneficial bilateral and multilateral trade relationships
Trade plus	Dense trade agreements and movement of talent toward the United States
Trust increase	Increase in public service and public trust
U.S. desirable	Strong dollar; the United States is a desirable global partner
U.S. grows	U.S. middle class grows; the United States has key trade agreements

References

Curry, Andrew, and Anthony Hodgson, "Seeing in Multiple Horizons: Connecting Futures to Strategy," *Journal of Futures Studies*, Vol. 13, No. 1, August 2008.

Dewar, James A., *Assumption-Based Planning: A Tool for Reducing Avoidable Surprises*, Cambridge University Press, 2002.

Dewey, John, *Freedom and Culture*, G. P. Putnam's Sons, 1939.

Ecola, Liisa, Steven W. Popper, Richard Silberglitt, and Laura Fraade-Blanar, *The Road to Zero: A Vision for Achieving Zero Roadway Deaths by 2050*, RAND Corporation, RR-2333-NSC, 2018. As of August 4, 2023:
https://www.rand.org/pubs/research_reports/RR2333.html

Georghiou, Luke, Jennifer Cassingena Harper, Michael Keenan, Ian Miles, and Rafael Popper, eds., *The Handbook of Technology Foresight: Concepts and Practice*, Edward Elgar Publishing, 2008.

Glenn, Jerome C., and the Futures Group International, "Scenarios," in Jerome C. Glenn and Theodore J. Gordon, eds., *Futures Research Methodology—Version 3.0*, The Millennium Project, 2009.

Gordon, Theodore J., "Interactive Scenarios," in Jerome C. Glenn and Theodore J. Gordon, eds., *Futures Research Methodology—Version 3.0*, The Millennium Project, 2009.

Holmes, Oliver Wendell, "The Chambered Nautilus," 1858.

Kahn, Herman, and Anthony J. Wiener, *The Year 2000: A Framework for Speculation on the Next Thirty-Three Years*, Macmillan, 1967.

Popper, Steven W., "Designing a Robust Decision–Based National Security Policy Process: Strategic Choices for Uncertain Times," in Aaron B. Frank and Elizabeth M. Bartels, eds., *Adaptive Engagement for Undergoverned Spaces: Concepts, Challenges, and Prospects for New Approaches*, RAND Corporation, RR-A1275-1, 2022. As of March 7, 2024:
https://www.rand.org/pubs/research_reports/RRA1275-1.html

Stern, Paul C., and Harvey V. Fineberg, eds., *Understanding Risk: Informing Decisions in a Democratic Society*, National Academy Press, 1996.

www.ingramcontent.com/pod-product-compliance
Lightning Source LLC
Chambersburg PA
CBHW080159290725
30129CB00015B/13
* 9 7 8 1 9 7 7 4 1 4 6 9 4 *